Native Americ

National Museum of the /
Smithsonian Institution

CW01478497

A POSTCARD PORTFOLIO

Hugh Lauter Levin Associates, Inc.

The Smithsonian Institution's National Museum of the American Indian, founded in 1989, is an invaluable resource for the preservation and celebration of the traditions and cultures of Native Americans.

In 1897, while supervising railroad construction in Arizona, George Gustav Heye bought a deerhide shirt from one of his Navajo foremen. When Heye died sixty years later, he'd spent his life and a $10 million fortune amassing the finest collection of American Indian materials in the world—one million objects representing Native cultures from the Arctic to Tierra del Fuego and spanning ten thousand years. The pieces included in this portfolio highlight this truly American collection—from a Kiowa headdress from Oklahoma to a Chilkat tunic from Alaska to a Miccosukee–Seminole doll from Florida.

Heye's marvelous collection is a cornerstone of the National Museum of the American Indian. Today, exhibitions of these objects provide a forum for Native peoples to interpret their cultures and experiences for a larger public. The museum's facilities— the Heye Center in New York; the Cultural Resources Center in Suitland, Maryland, opening in 1998; and the museum on the National Mall in Washington, D.C., opening in 2002—have been designed in consultation with Native peoples to be centers for educational programs, ceremonies, and live presentations.

In addition, community services, including collaborations with Native individuals and organizations and outreach through publications, recordings, and a site on the World Wide Web, provide broad access to the museum's resources. Through these programs and services, the museum works to present the living cultures of the Americas and to share something of what it means to be Indian.

Haida dance rattle, c. 1850–1875
Skidegate, Queen Charlotte Island, British Columbia, Canada
Carved cedar wood
Length: 32.5 cm
Photo by Pam Dewey
National Museum of the American Indian, 1.8028
© 1997 Smithsonian Institution

Published by Hugh Lauter Levin Associates, Inc.

Pomo coiled-weave basket with interwoven glass beads
California
Diameter: 23.75 cm
Photo by Karen Furth
National Museum of the American Indian, 4.8782
© 1997 Smithsonian Institution

Published by Hugh Lauter Levin Associates, Inc.

Minneconjou Sioux painted dance shield depicting
a battle between Sioux and Absaroke (Crow) warriors.
The man in the center is Hump, a famous chief.
South Dakota
Painted cowhide
Diameter: 55 cm
Photo by David Heald
National Museum of the American Indian, 6.2195
© 1997 Smithsonian Institution

Published by Hugh Lauter Levin Associates, Inc.

Seneca *gustoweh* (headdress)
Ontario, Canada
Leather with silver band, wampum beads, and feathers
50.7 x 61 cm
Photo by David Heald
National Museum of the American Indian, 6.354
© 1997 Smithsonian Institution

Published by Hugh Lauter Levin Associates, Inc.

Navajo *beeldléí* (blanket), 1825–1860
Handspun wool and raveled yarn
172.2 x 132.6 cm
Photo by David Heald
National Museum of the American Indian, 9.1912
© 1997 Smithsonian Institution

Published by Hugh Lauter Levin Associates, Inc.

Unangan (Aleut) basket and cover, late 19th century
Alaska
Wild rye beach grass (?), silk thread
Height: 19 cm
Photo by David Heald
National Museum of the American Indian, 9.7038
© 1997 Smithsonian Institution

Published by Hugh Lauter Levin Associates, Inc.

Huron tobacco case
Canada
Birch bark with moosehair
10 x 5.5 cm
Photo by Karen Furth
National Museum of the American Indian, 10.7448
© 1997 Smithsonian Institution

Published by Hugh Lauter Levin Associates, Inc.

Published by Hugh Lauter Levin Associates, Inc.

Sioux beaded deerskin
South Dakota
115.5 x 185 cm
Photo by David Heald
National Museum of the American Indian, 11.1739
© 1997 Smithsonian Institution

Published by Hugh Lauter Levin Associates, Inc.

Pima basket tray
Arizona
Plant fibers
Diameter: 24.8 cm
Photo by David Heald
National Museum of the American Indian, 11.415
© 1997 Smithsonian Institution

Published by Hugh Lauter Levin Associates, Inc.

Letter written by "Big Bow", Kiowa Chief, and Sergeant of
a Detachment of Kiowa Scouts serving at Camp on the
Sweetwater, informing the Kiowa Scouts serving at
Fort Sill, that they are all well and ready to go on the
War-path. Their Squaws are also well.

Letter and drawing by Chief Big Bow, a sergeant
of a detachment of Kiowa scouts on the Sweetwater,
to a similar group at Fort Sill, c. 1875.
Oklahoma
20.5 x 31 cm
Photo by David Heald
National Museum of the American Indian, 11.8347
© 1997 Smithsonian Institution

Published by Hugh Lauter Levin Associates, Inc.

Lenape (Delaware) bag
Eastern Woodlands
Deerhide with quills, tin cones, and feathers
28.5 x 21.3 cm
Photo by David Heald
National Museum of the American Indian, 13.5886
© 1997 Smithsonian Institution

Published by Hugh Lauter Levin Associates, Inc.

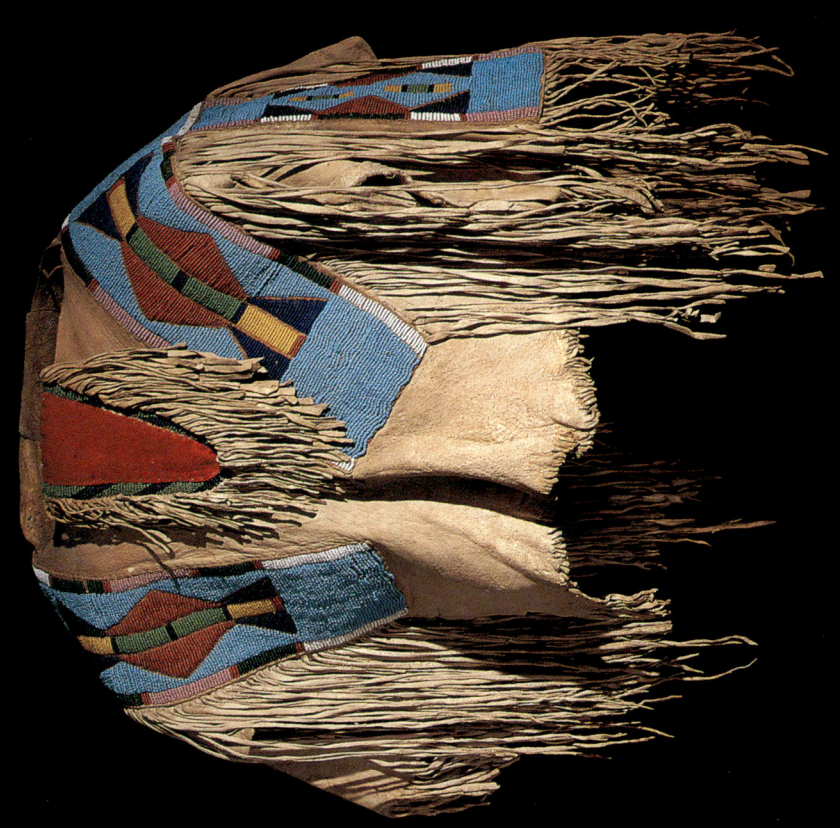

Absaroke (Crow) child's shirt
Montana
Hide, with beads and wool
Length: 42 cm
Photo by David Heald
National Museum of the American Indian, 13.7133
© 1997 Smithsonian Institution

Published by Hugh Lauter Levin Associates, Inc.

Aivilingmiut Iglulik *amautik* (woman's parka), early 20th century
Near Chesterfield Inlet, Canada
Caribou hide with fur lining, glass beads, ivory toggles
Length: 123.5 cm
Photo by David Heald
National Museum of the American Indian, 13.7198
© 1997 Smithsonian Institution

Published by Hugh Lauter Levin Associates, Inc.

Absaroke (Crow) headdress
Montana
Owl and eagle feathers, wool trade cloth, and buffalo hide
142 x 33 cm
Photo by David Heald
National Museum of the American Indian, 15.2393
© 1997 Smithsonian Institution

Published by Hugh Lauter Levin Associates, Inc.

Haida hat
British Columbia, Canada
Woven, painted spruce root and carved, painted wood
Height: 44.4 cm
Photo by David Heald
National Museum of the American Indian, 15.4313

Published by Hugh Lauter Levin Associates, Inc.

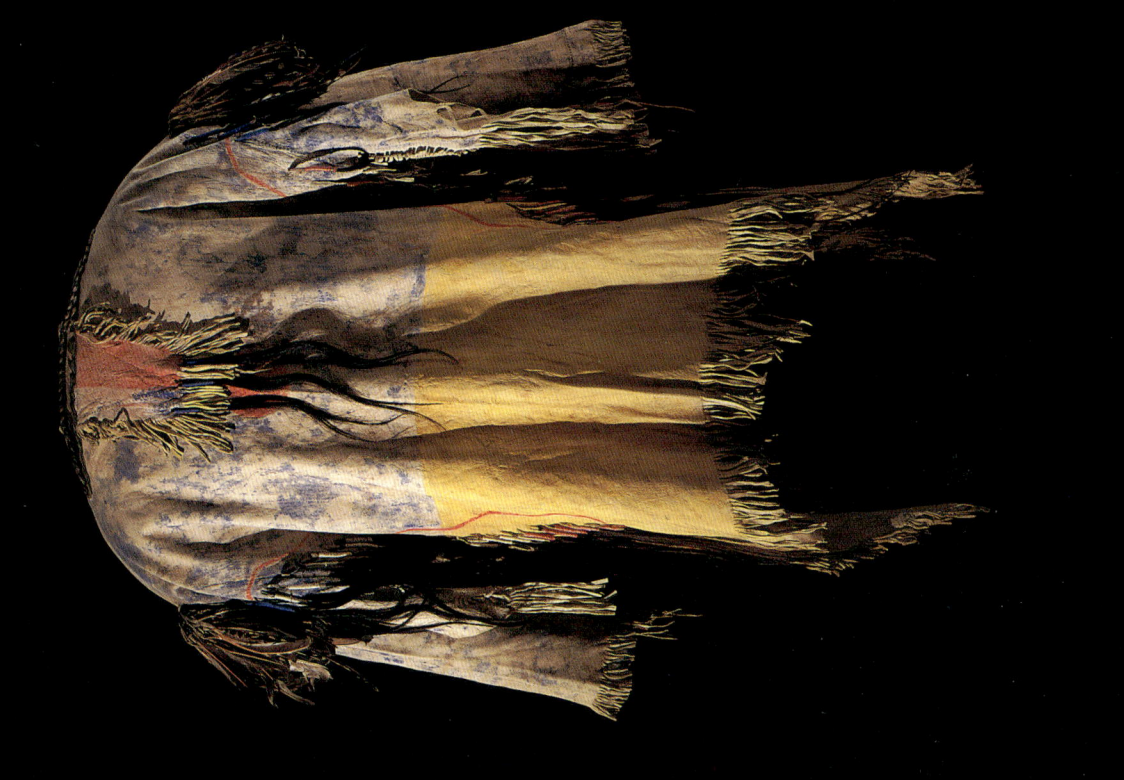

Shirt worn by Crazy Horse
Oglala Lakota
Hide with paint, scalp locks, and woodpecker feathers
Length: 84 cm
Photo by David Heald
National Museum of the American Indian, 16.1351
© 1997 Smithsonian Institution

Published by Hugh Lauter Levin Associates, Inc.

White Mountain Apache shield cover
Arizona
Deerhide and pigment
Diameter: 47.6 cm
Photo by David Heald
National Museum of the American Indian, 18.4403
© 1997 Smithsonian Institution

Published by Hugh Lauter Levin Associates, Inc.

Miccosukee–Seminole man's *foksikco.bi* (big shirt), c. 1925–1935
Florida
Length: 132 cm
Photo by David Heald
National Museum of the American Indian, 19.5115
© 1997 Smithsonian Institution

Published by Hugh Lauter Levin Associates, Inc.

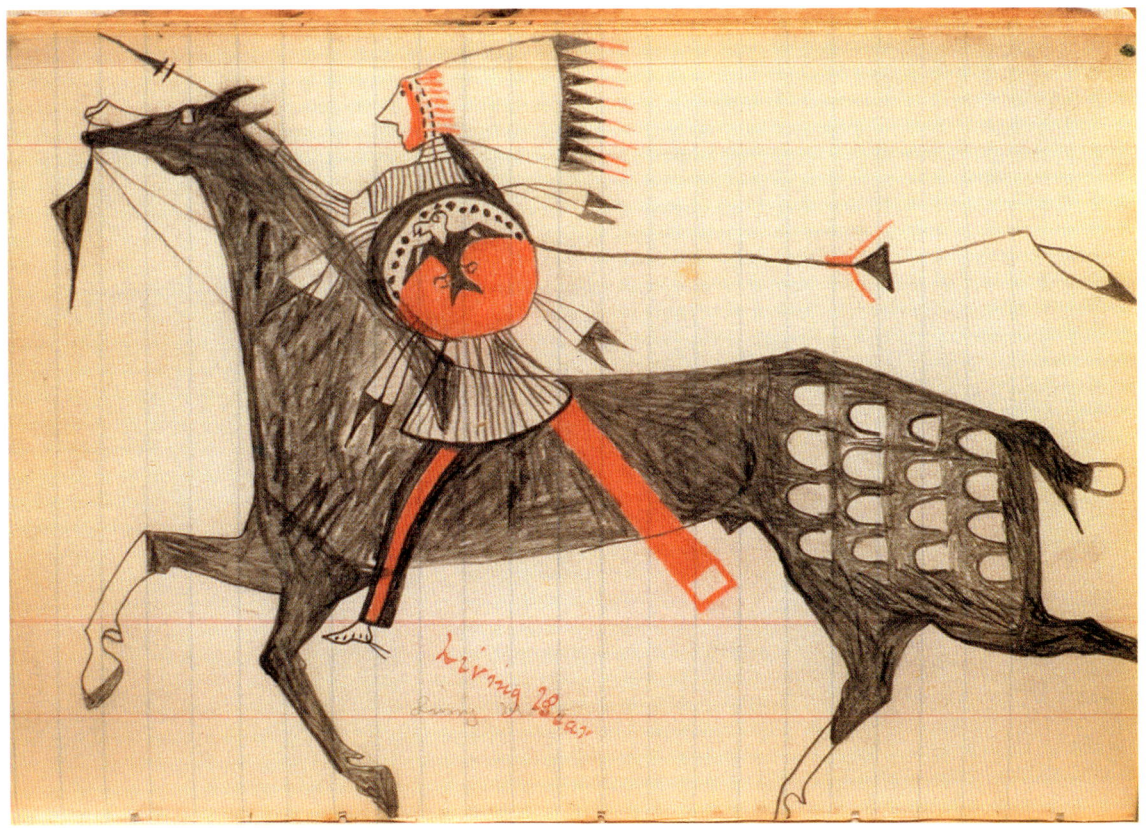

Living Bear

Image from a book of drawings by Red Dog (Lakota), late 19th century
South Dakota
Crayon and ink on paper
12.7 x 19.1 cm
Photo by Pam Dewey
National Museum of the American Indian, 20.6230
© 1997 Smithsonian Institution

Published by Hugh Lauter Levin Associates, Inc.

Dress, late 19th/early 20th century
Southern Plains
Length: 140 cm
Photo by David Heald
National Museum of the American Indian, 20.8052
© 1997 Smithsonian Institution

Published by Hugh Lauter Levin Associates, Inc.

Navajo *beeldléí* (blanket), c. 1875
Handspun wool and raveled yarn
160.8 x 188.2 cm
Photo by David Heald
National Museum of the American Indian, 21.4886
© 1997 Smithsonian Institution

Published by Hugh Lauter Levin Associates, Inc.

Miccosukee–Seminole doll, c. 1935
Florida
Palmetto fiber, embroidery floss, cloth, beads
Height: 38.1 cm
Photo by David Heald
National Museum of the American Indian, 22.1549
© 1997 Smithsonian Institution

Published by Hugh Lauter Levin Associates, Inc.

Navajo *beeldléí* (blanket), 1880–1890
Handspun wool and commercial yarn
152.4 x 143.5 cm
Photo by David Heald
National Museum of the American Indian, 25.3708
© 1997 Smithsonian Institution

Published by Hugh Lauter Levin Associates, Inc.

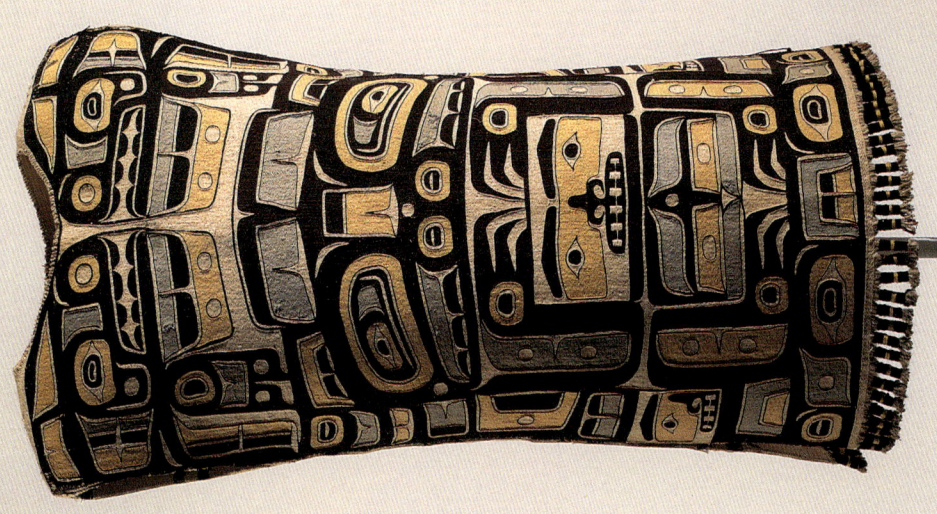

Chilkat Tlingit tunic with bear design, 19th century
Alaska
Goat wool and cedar bark
Length: 96 cm
Photo by David Heald
National Museum of the American Indian, 7076
© 1997 Smithsonian Institution

Published by Hugh Lauter Levin Associates, Inc.

Absaroke (Crow) sword scabbard, late 19th century
Montana
134 x 64 cm
Photo by David Heald
National Museum of the American Indian, 8480
© 1997 Smithsonian Institution

Published by Hugh Lauter Levin Associates, Inc.

Sioux double-handle horn spoon
Length: 20.3 cm
Photo by David Heald
National Museum of the American Indian, 9068
© 1997 Smithsonian Institution

Published by Hugh Lauter Levin Associates, Inc.